BRIAN LARA

WEST INDIES CRICKETER

MR VIVEK KUMAR PANDEY

Made with ♥ on the Notion Press Platform
www.notionpress.com

Contents

Foreword

Short Biography Of Brian Lara & Life Style, Career etc. During Writing This Book No Character, No Religion & No Caste Are Harmed. It's Only For Study Purpose.

Preface

Author biography in English :

MY NAME IS VIVEK KUMAR PANDEY . I WAS BORN IN 30 SEP 2002,I AM FROM SURAT GUJARAT INDIA.MY DREAM WAS TO BE GOOD WRITERS ,MY FAMILY SUPPORTED ME TO SUCCESSFUL AND I CAN DO IT MY SELF.How do I write? That is a question, I believe, that can be honestly answered by me."CELEBRATING YOUNGEST WRITER AWARD WINNER IN GUJARAT 1ST RANK" MR PANDEY JI . I may think I did a good job writing something. The reader is the one who decides the quality of my writing. I do find writing to be natural to me and therefore find it to be a real challenge. My trick as a challenged writer is to do the best I can and know that I am happy with the final outcome. It may take a while to do my best and there may be quite a few problems I run into along the way.

I am not a greedy person those who are thinking about me and my self I never tried it anyone people suffering from sadness ,I trying to get promoted people suffering from happiness and joy in your Life Time. Now in current situation in India and also world people are unemployed and have no many but our indian governor help to people to get free food from ration card , i also take part in leadership team ,i am Motivational speaker , Film script writer. There was my two dream firstly writer and secondly actor & also my own film is upcoming soon i done almost completely completed script for my film .I AM GOING TO SAY WORD OF HEART TOUCH OUT PLEASE READ IT" , firstly i thanks my father he supports me in this field they always getting inspired me by own his words and behavior ,they always said that he was a biggest person in the world in future and also they purchase fruit and chocolate for me in anytime & anyway , firstly my father buy him then call me Vivek you want a chocolate i will say yes papa but how many tell me ,papa: you tell me how much i buy him i told 1 or 2 chocolate but my father purchase whole the boxes of chocolate and they get suprised me. MY FATHER WAS BORN IN " 20 SEPTEMBER" 1971 IN INDIA.

1) MY FATHER FAVORITE CLOTHES IS KURTA PAIJMA AND ALSO STYLES SHOE

2) FAVORITE SINGER IS KISHORE DA

3) FAVORITE STATE GUJARAT AND KOLKATA , HIS VILLAGE IN BIHAR

4) FAVORITE COLOR BLACK AND WHITE

THEY ALSO LOVE cricket like IPL and one day t-20 .they also like watching a News daily and heard the song daily ,they also interested in tik tok video but in current time tik tok is banned in india but also few videos are in you tube. In lockdown time my family and me very enjoy day daily. my father play daily ludo with his sister and son, daughter.they always loved tea and coffee anytime call me ". I make it tea for my father but some reason after the April to june they are suffering from fever and cough , weakness on 6 June 2020 my father death. they not told me say bye bye his life. After death of 6 June on 10 june my mom and dad anniversary.but my father is Best in the world they can do anything for me please take care of father and respect it of your parents.

ONE

BRIAN LARA

- **Brian Lara**

1. Short Biography Brian Lara Of & Life Style, Career etc. During Writing This Book No Character, No Religion & No Caste Are Harmed. It's Only For Study Purpose.

Brian Charles Lara, (born 2 May 1969) is a Trinidadian former international cricketer, widely acknowledged as one of the greatest batsmen of all time. He topped the Test batting rankings on several occasions and holds several cricketing records, including the record for the highest individual score in first-class cricket, with 501 not out for Warwickshire against Durham at Edgbaston in 1994, which is the only quintuple-hundred in first-class cricket history.

Lara also holds the record for the highest individual score in a Test innings after scoring 400 not out at Antigua during the 4th test against England in 2004. Lara also held the record of scoring the highest number of runs in a single over in a Test match for 18 years when he scored 28 runs off an over by Robin Peterson of South Africa in 2003 (overtaken by Jasprit Bumrah in 2022).

Lara's match-winning performance of 153 not out against Australia in Bridgetown, Barbados in 1999 has been rated by Wisden as the second-best batting performance in the history of Test cricket, next only to the 270 runs scored by Sir Donald Bradman in The Ashes Test match of 1937. Muttiah Muralitharan has hailed Lara as his toughest opponent among all batsmen in the world. Lara was awarded the Wisden Leading Cricketer in the World awards in 1994 and 1995 and is also one of only three cricketers to receive the BBC Overseas Sports Personality of the Year, the other two being Sir Garfield Sobers and Shane Warne.

Brian Lara was appointed honorary member of the Order of Australia on 27 November 2009. In September 2012 he was inducted to the ICC's Hall of Fame as a 2012–13 season inductee. In 2013, Lara received Honorary Life Membership of the MCC becoming the 31st West Indian to receive the honor.

Brian Lara is popularly nicknamed as "The Prince of Port of Spain" or simply "The Prince". He has the dubious distinction of playing in the second-highest number of test matches (63) in which his team was on the losing side, just behind Shivnarine Chanderpaul (68).

- **Brian Lara life**

Brian is one of eleven siblings. His father Bunty and one of his older sisters Agnes Cyrus enrolled him in the local Harvard Coaching Clinic at the age of six for weekly coaching sessions on Sundays. As a result, Lara had a very early education in correct batting technique. Lara's first school was St. Joseph's Roman Catholic primary. He then went to San Juan Secondary School, which is located on

Moreau Road, Lower Santa Cruz. A year later, at fourteen years old, he moved on to Fatima College where he started his development as a promising young player under cricket coach Harry Ramdass. Aged 14, he amassed 745 runs in the schoolboys‘ league, with an average of 126.16 per innings, which earned him selection for the Trinidad national under-16 team. When he was 15 years old, he played in his first West Indian under-19 youth tournament and that same year, Lara represented West Indies in Under-19 cricket.

- **Brian Lara Cricket career**

1987 was a breakthrough year for Lara, when in the West Indies Youth Championships he scored 498 runs breaking the record of 480 by Carl Hooper set the previous year. He captained the tournament-winning Trinidad and Tobago, who profited from a match-winning 116 from Lara.

In January 1988, Lara made his first-class debut for Trinidad and Tobago in the Red Stripe Cup against Leeward Islands. In his second first-class match he made 92 against a Barbados attack containing Joel Garner and Malcolm Marshall, two greats of West Indies teams. Later in the same year, he captained the West Indies team in Australia for the Bicentennial Youth World Cup where the West Indies reached the semi-finals. Later that year, his innings of 182 as captain of the West Indies Under-23s against the touring Indian team further elevated his reputation.

His first selection for the full West Indies team followed in due course, but unfortunately coincided with the death of his father and Lara withdrew from the team. In 1989, he captained a West Indies B Team in Zimbabwe and scored 145.

In 1990, at the age of 20, Lara became Trinidad and Tobago's youngest-ever captain, leading them that season to victory in the one-day Geddes Grant Shield. It was also in 1990 that he made his belated Test debut for West Indies against Pakistan, scoring 44 and 5. He had made his ODI debut a month earlier against Pakistan, scoring 11.

- **Brian Lara International career**

In January 1993, Lara scored 277 versus Australia in Sydney. This, his maiden Test century in his fifth Test, was the turning point of the series as West Indies won the final two Tests to win the series 2–1. Lara went on to name his daughter Sydney after scoring 277 at SCG.

Lara holds several world records for high scoring. He has the highest individual score in both first-class cricket (501 not out for Warwickshire against Durham in 1994) and Test cricket (400 not out for the West Indies against England in 2004). Lara amassed his world record 501 in 474 minutes off only 427 balls. He hit 308 in boundaries (10 sixes and 62 fours). His partners were Roger Twose (115 partnership – 2nd wicket), Trevor Penney (314 – 3rd), Paul Smith (51 – 4th) and Keith Piper (322 unbroken – 5th). Earlier in that season Lara scored six centuries in seven innings while playing for Warwickshire.

He is the only man to have reclaimed the Test record score, having scored 375 against England in 1994, a record that stood until Matthew Hayden's 380 against Zimbabwe in 2003. His 400 not out also made him the second player (after Donald Bradman) to score two Test triple-centuries, and the second to score two first-class quadruple-centuries. He has scored nine double-centuries in Test cricket, third after Bradman's twelve and Kumar Sangakkara's eleven. As a captain, he scored five double-centuries, which is the highest by any one who is in charge. In 1995 Lara in the Test match away series against England, scored 3 hundreds in three consecutive Matches which earned him the Man of the Series award. The Test Series was eventually drawn 2–2. He also held the record for the highest total number of runs in a Test career, after overtaking Allan Border in an innings of 226 played at Adelaide Oval, Australia in November 2005. This was later broken by Sachin Tendulkar of India on 17 October 2008 whilst playing against Australia at Mohali in the 2nd Test of the Border–Gavaskar Trophy 2008.

Lara captained the West Indies from 1998 to 1999, when West Indies suffered their first whitewash at the hands of South Africa. Following this they played Australia in a four-Test series which was drawn 2–2, with Lara scoring 546 runs including three centuries and one double hundred. In the second Test at Kingston he scored 213 while in the third Test he scored 153* in the second innings as West Indies chased down 311 with one wicket left. He won the Man of the Match award for both matches and was also named Man of the Series.

The Wisden 100 rates Lara's 153 not out against Australia in Bridgetown in 1998–99 as the second-best innings ever after Sir Donald Bradman's 270 against England in Melbourne in 1936–37.

In 2001 Lara was named the Man of the Carlton Series in Australia with an average of 46.50, the highest average by a West Indian in that series, scoring two half centuries and one century, 116 against Australia. That same year Lara amassed 688 runs in the three match away Test series against Sri Lanka making three centuries, and one fifty—including the double-century and a century in the first and second innings of the 3rd Test match at the

Sinhalese Sports Ground, equating to 42% of the team's runs in that series. These extraordinary performances led Muttiah Muralitharan to state that Lara was the most dangerous batsman he had ever bowled to.

Lara was reappointed as captain against the touring Australians in 2003, and struck 110 in his first Test match back in charge, showing a return to stellar performance. Later that season, under his captaincy, West Indies won the two match Test series against Sri Lanka 1–0 with Lara making a double-century in the First Test. In September 2004, West Indies won the ICC Champions Trophy in England under his captaincy. For his performances in 2004, he was named both in the World Test XI and ODI XI by ICC.

In March 2005, Lara declined selection for the West Indies team because of a dispute over his personal Cable & Wireless sponsorship deal, which clashed with the Cricket Board's main sponsor, Digicel. Six other players were involved in this dispute, including stars Chris Gayle, Ramnaresh Sarwan and Dwayne Bravo. Lara said he declined selection in a stand of solidarity, when these players were dropped because of their sponsorship deals. The issue was resolved after the first Test of the series against the touring South African team.Lara returned to the team for the second Test (and scored a huge first innings score of 196), but in the process lost his captaincy indefinitely to the newly appointed Shivnarine Chanderpaul. In the next Test, against the same opponents, he scored a 176 in the first innings. After a one-day series against South Africa, he scored his first Test century against the visiting Pakistanis in the first Test at Kensington Oval, Bridgetown, Barbados which the West Indies eventually won.

On 26 April 2006 Lara was reappointed the captain of the West Indies cricket team for the third time. This followed the resignation of Shivnarine Chanderpaul, who had been captain for thirteen months—in which the West Indies won just one of the 14 Test matches they had competed. In May 2006, Lara led the West Indies to successful One-Day series victories against Zimbabwe and India. Lara's team played Australia in the finals of the DLF Cup and the ICC Champions Trophy where they finished runners up in both finals.

On 16 December 2006 he became the first player for the West Indies to pass 10,000 One Day International runs, and, along with Sachin Tendulkar, one of only two players, at the time, to do so in both forms of the game. On 10 April 2007 Lara confirmed his retirement from one-day cricket post the 2007 Cricket World Cup. A few days later he announced that he would in fact be retiring from all international cricket after the tournament.Lara played his final international game on 21 April 2007 in a dead rubber World Cup game against England. He was run out for 18 after a mix-up with Marlon Samuels; England won the game by 1 wicket. Before the end of this World Cup Glenn McGrath stated that Lara is the greatest batsman that he has ever bowled to.

- **Brian Lara Retirement**

On 19 April 2007 Lara announced his retirement from all forms of international cricket, indicating that the West Indies vs England match on 21 April 2007 would be his last international appearance. He was run out after a bad mixup with Marlon Samuels for 18, as England went on to win the match by one wicket.

He announced before the 2007 Cricket World Cup that this would be his last appearance in One Day Internationals. After his last match, in the post-game presentation interview, he asked the fans, "Did I entertain?", to which he received a resounding cheer from the crowd, after which he went out and took his 'lap of honour' where he met and shook hands with many of the fans. Lara stated this would be his last appearance in international cricket, he has also indicated his interest in retaining some involvement in the sport.

On 23 July 2007 Lara agreed to sign for the Indian Cricket League. He is the former captain of the Mumbai Champs. He volunteered to play for his home team Trinidad during the start of 2008 domestic season. He had not played for Trinidad for the last two years. He made his comeback a memorable one with a match winning hundred over Guyana, followed by a dismissive undefeated half-century in the second innings, scored at over two runs per ball. In the third-round game.

Lara suffered a fractured arm against the Leeward Islands in St Maarten on 19 January, which kept him out of the ICL season. He nevertheless affirmed his commitment to returning to Twenty20 cricket, and on 27 June 2010 appeared for the Marylebone Cricket Club match against a touring Pakistan team, scoring 37 from 32 balls.In 2012, Lara became involved with the Bangladesh Premier League team Chittagong Kings as their brand ambassador.

On the occasion of bicentennial anniversary of Lord's ground he played for the team of MCC, under the leadership of Sachin Tendulkar against the Rest of World XI in a 50 over game. He went on to score a half century in an eventual win for the MCC.

- **Brian Lara in 2010 return**

After negotiations between Surrey and Lara for the 2010 Friends Provident t20 failed to come to anything, Lara declared that he still wanted to sign a contract to play Twenty20 cricket. Late in the year he joined Southern Rocks, a Zimbabwean side, to compete in the 2010–11 Stanbic Bank 20 Series. On his debut for the Rocks, and his first-ever Twenty20 match, he scored a half-century, top-scoring for the Rocks with 65. He added 34 runs in his next two innings, but then left the competition, citing "commitments elsewhere".

After expressing his interest to play in the 2011 fourth edition of the Indian Premier League (IPL), and despite not having played active cricket for four years, Brian Lara still managed to attract the highest reserve price of $400,000 ahead of the IPL players' auction in early January 2011. however, no franchise bought him.

In July 2014, he played for the MCC side in the Bicentenary Celebration match at Lord's.On 18 November 2016, Brian Lara signed with Newcastle C&S D5's side The Bennett Hotel Centurions.

- **Brian Lara Coaching**

In December 2021 Brian Lara was appointed as Batting Coach and Strategic Advisor of the Sunrisers Hyderabad team for the IPL 2022 edition.

- **Brian Lara Personal life**

1. Lara's father died in 1989 of a heart attack. His mother died in 2002 of cancer.

2. Barack Obama and Lara during the US President's tour of Trinidad and Tobago in 2009. Obama had asked to meet Lara, whom he described as the "Michael Jordan of cricket".
3. Lara has two daughters whom he fathered with Trinidadian journalist and model Leasel Rovedas. Lara has dated former British lingerie model Lynnsey Ward.
4. In 2009, Lara was made an honorary Member of the Order of Australia (AM) for services to West Indian and Australian cricket.
5. Lara will be one of four persons to receive the highest award of the Caribbean Community (Caricom) in July. Lara received an honorary doctorate from the University of Sheffield on Wednesday 10 January 2007. The ceremony took place at the Trinidad Hilton, Port of Spain, Trinidad and Tobago.
6. In September 2009, Lara was inducted as an honorary lifetime member of the Royal St. Kitts Golf Club.
7. On 29 October 2011 Lara was conferred with an honorary doctorate of laws by the University of the West Indies, St Augustine.
8. On 14 September 2012 he was inducted to the ICC's Hall of Fame at the awards ceremony held in Colombo, Sri Lanka as a 2012–13 season inductee.
9. The Brian Lara Stadium, in Trinidad and Tobago, opened in 2017, was named in his honour.
10. On 4 July 2019 Lara was bestowed with an honorary doctorate by the D Y Patil International University of India.
11. On 7 September 2008 he took part in Soccer Aid 2008, and on 6 June 2010 in Soccer Aid 2010, playing for the Rest of the World vs a team of England celebrities and ex-pros. Lara was also a talented football player in his

youth and often played with his close friends Dwight Yorke, Shaka Hislop and Russell Latapy while growing up together in Trinidad. Yorke, Hislop and Latapy would go on to play for Trinidad and Tobago at the 2006 FIFA World Cup.

- **Brian Lara Records**

1. Lara struck 277 runs against Australia in Sydney, his maiden Test century, the fourth-highest maiden Test century by any batsman, the highest individual score in all Tests between the two teams and the fourth-highest century ever recorded against Australia by any Test batsman.
2. He became the first man to score seven centuries in eight first-class innings, the first being the record 375 against England and the last being the record 501 not out against Durham.
3. After Matthew Hayden had eclipsed his Test record for highest individual score 375 by five runs in 2003, he reclaimed the record scoring 400 not out in 2004 against England. With these innings he became the second player to score two Test triple-centuries, the first & only player to score two 350-plus scores in test history, the second player to score two career quadruple-centuries after Bill Ponsford, the only player to achieve both these milestones, and regained the distinction of being the holder of both the record first-class individual innings and the record Test individual innings. He is the only player to break the world record twice.
4. He also set the record for the highest individual test score as captain (400*)

5. In the same innings, he became the second batsman to score 1,000 Test runs in five different years, four days after Matthew Hayden first set the record.
6. He was the all-time leading run scorer in Test cricket, a record he attained on 26 November 2005 until surpassed by Sachin Tendulkar on 17 October 2008.
7. He was the fastest batsman to score 10,000 (with Sachin Tendulkar) and 11,000 Test runs, in terms of number of innings.
8. He scored 34 Test centuries; joint-fifth along with Sunil Gavaskar, on the all-time list behind Sachin Tendulkar (51), Jacques Kallis (45), Ricky Ponting (41) and Rahul Dravid (36).
9. He has the most centuries for a West Indian
10. Nine of his centuries are double-centuries (surpassed only by Kumar Sangakkara and Donald Bradman)
11. Two of them are triple-centuries (matched by Australia's Donald Bradman, India's Virender Sehwag, and West Indies' Chris Gayle).
12. He has scored centuries against all Test-playing nations. He achieved this feat in 2005 by scoring his first Test century against Pakistan at the Kensington Oval in Bridgetown, Barbados.
13. He became the sixth batsman to score a century in one session, doing so against Pakistan on 21 November 2006.
14. Lara has scored 20% of his team runs, a feat surpassed only by Bradman (23%) and George Headley (21%). Lara scored 688 runs (42% of team output, a record for a series of three or more Tests, and the second-highest aggregate runs in history for a three-Test series) in the 2001–02 tour of Sri Lanka.
15. He also scored a century and a double-century in the third Test in that same Sri Lanka tour, a feat repeated

only five other times in Test cricket history.

16. He has scored the most runs (351) on a losing side in a Test.
17. He scored the largest proportion (53.83 per cent) of his team's runs in a Test (221 out of 390 and 130 out of 262). He eclipsed the long-standing record of 51.88 per cent by the South African J. H. Sinclair (106 out of 177 and 4 out of 35) against England at Cape Town in an 1898–1899 series.
18. Lara holds the world record of scoring most runs in a single over (28 runs against left-arm spinner RJ Peterson of South Africa) in Test cricket. He also scored 26 runs in a single over off the bowling of Danish Kaneria at Multan Cricket Stadium on 21 November 2006.
19. He scored the ninth-fastest Test century, doing so off 77 balls against Pakistan on 21 November 2006.
20. With 164 catches, he is the eighth-highest all-time catch-taker of non-wicketkeepers, behind Rahul Dravid, Mahela Jayawardene, Jacques Kallis, Ricky Ponting, Mark Waugh, Stephen Fleming and Graeme Smith.
21. In 1994, he was awarded the BBC Sports Personality of the Year Overseas Personality Award. In 1995, he was chosen as one of the Wisden Cricketers of the Year.
22. Lara had played some of his best innings in the latter stage of his career. Wisden published a top 100 list in July 2001, a distillation of the best performances from 1,552 Tests, 54,494 innings and 29,730 bowling performances. Three innings by Lara were placed in the top 15 (the most for any batsman in that range). His 153 not out in Bridgetown, Barbados, during West Indies' 2–2 home series draw against Australia in *1998–1999 was deemed the second-greatest Test innings ever played, behind Bradman's 270 against England in the Third Test of the

1936–1937 series at Melbourne.

23. He was voted as second-scariest batsman to face in the "World's Scariest Batsman" poll of international bowlers

TWO

HISTORY OF THE WEST INDIES CRICKET TEAM

- **History of the West Indies cricket team**

The history of the West Indian cricket team begins in the 1880s when the first combined West Indian team was formed and toured Canada and the United States. In the 1890s, the first representative sides were selected to play visiting English sides. Administered by the West Indies Cricket Board ("WICB"), and known colloquially as The Windies, the West Indies cricket team represents a sporting confederation of English-speaking Caribbean countries.

The WICB joined the sport's international ruling body, the Imperial Cricket Conference, in 1926, and played their first official international match, which in cricket is called a Test, in 1928.Although blessed with some great players in their early days as a Test nation, their successes remained sporadic until the 1960s, by which time the side had changed from a white-dominated to a black-dominated side. By the late 1970s, the West Indies had a side recognised as unofficial world champions, a title they retained throughout the 1980s.

Their team from the 1970s and 1980s is now widely regarded as having been one of the best in test cricket's history, alongside Don Bradman's Invincibles. During these glory years, the Windies were noted for their four-man fast bowling attack, backed up by some of the best batsmen in the world. The 1980s saw them set a then-record streak of 11 consecutive Test victories in 1984, which was part of a still-standing record of 27 tests without defeat , as well as inflicting two 5–0 "blackwashes" against the old enemy of England. Throughout the 1990s and 2000s, however, West Indian cricket declined, in part due to the rise in popularity of athletics and football in West Indian countries, and the team today is struggling to regain its past glory.

In their early days in the 1930s, the side represented the British colonies of the West Indies Federation plus British Guyana. The current side represents the now independent states of Antigua and Barbuda, Barbados, Dominica, Grenada, Guyana, Jamaica, Saint Kitts and Nevis, Saint Lucia, Saint Vincent and the Grenadines and Trinidad and Tobago, and the British dependencies of Anguilla, Montserrat and the British Virgin Islands along with the U.S. Virgin Islands and St. Maarten.National teams also exist for the various islands, which, as they are all separate countries, very much keep their local identities and support their local favourites. These national teams take part in the West Indian first-class competition, the Stanford 20/20, the Carib Beer Cup . It is also common for other international teams to play the island teams for warm-up games before they take on the combined West Indies team.

- **tours**

The first major international cricket played in the West Indies was between local, often predominantly white, sides and English tourists – the Middlesex player Robert Slade Lucas toured the West Indies with a team in 1894–95, and two years later Arthur Priestley took a team to Barbados, Trinidad, and Jamaica, which included, for the first time, a match against a side styled "All West Indies", which the West Indians won. Lord Hawke's English team, including several English Test players, toured around the same time, playing Trinidad, Barbados and British Guiana (now Guyana).

Then in 1900 the white Trinidadian Aucher Warner, the brother of future England captain Pelham Warner, led a touring side to England, but none of the matches on this tour were given first-class status. Two winters later, in 1901–02, the Hampshire wicketkeeper Richard Bennett's XI went to the West Indies, and played three games against teams styled as the "West Indies", which the hosts won 2–1. In 1904–05, Lord Brackley's XI toured the Caribbean – winning both its games against "West Indies".

The tours to England continued in 1906 when Harold Austin led a West Indian side to England. His side played a number of county teams, and drew their game against an "England XI". However, that England XI only included one contemporary Test player – wicketkeeper Dick Lilley – and he had not been on England's most recent tour, their 1905–6 tour of South Africa. The Marylebone Cricket Club, which had taken over responsibility for arranging all official overseas England tours, visited the West Indies in 1910–11, and 1912–13 but after that there was no international cricket of any note until the West Indian team went to England in 1923. This tour did not include a game against an England team, but there was an end-of-season game against HDG Leveson-Gower's XI against a virtual England Test side at the Scarborough cricket festival, a traditional end-of-season game against a touring side at the English seaside resort of Scarborough, which Leveson-Gower's XI won by only four wickets. 1925–26 saw another MCC tour of the West Indies.

The MCC was eager to promote cricket throughout the British Empire, and on 31 May 1926 the West Indian Cricket Board, along with their New Zealand and Indian counterparts, was elected to the Imperial Cricket Conference (ICC), which previously consisted of the MCC and representatives of Australia and South Africa. Election to full membership of the ICC meant the West Indies could play official Test matches, which is the designation given to the most important international games, and the Windies became the fourth team actually to play a recognised Test match on 23 June 1928 when they took on England at Lord's in London.They did not, however, enjoy immediate success – the West Indies lost all three 3-day Tests in that 1928 tour by a long way, failing to score 250 runs in any of their six innings in that series. They also failed to dismiss England for under 350 runs in a series completely dominated by England.

- **The early Tests (1930s and 1940s)**

The West Indies team that toured Australia in 1930–31.The West Indies played 19 Tests in the 1930s in four series against England and one against Australia. The first four of these were played against an England team led by the Honourable Freddie Calthorpe that toured in 1929–30.

However, as Harold Gilligan was leading another English team to New Zealand at exactly the same time, this was not a full-strength England side. The series ended one-all, with the West Indies first ever Test victory being recorded on 26 February 1930. West Indian George Headley scored the most runs (703) in the rubber and Learie Constantine took the most wickets (18).

The West Indies toured Australia in 1930–31. They lost the Test series 4–1. The fifth and final Test showed some promise – batting first, the West Indies spent the first three days earning a 250-run lead with five wickets down in their second innings. A bold declaration was backed up by their bowlers, as Herman Griffith took four wickets and West Indies won by 30 runs to their first overseas Test victory. By the time the team left, they had left a good impression of themselves with the Australian public, although at first the team were faced with several cultural differences – for example, their hosts did not at first appreciate that the tourists' Roman Catholic beliefs would mean they would refuse to play golf on Sundays or engage in more ribald behaviour.

The West Indian sides of the time were always led by white men, and the touring party to Australia comprised seven whites and eleven "natives", and the West Indian Board of Control wrote to their Australian counterparts saying "that all should reside at the same hotels". Australia at the time had in place its "White Australia" policy, with the Australian Board having to guarantee to the Government that the non-whites would leave at the end of the tour. When the West Indians arrived in Sydney, the whites were immediately given a different hotel from the blacks. They complained, and thereafter their wishes were met. The tour lost a lot of money, part of which was due to the Great

Depression then affecting Australia. The West Indians won four and lost eight of their 14 first-class fixtures.

1933 saw another tour of England. Their hosts had just come back from defeating Australia in the infamous Bodyline series, where England's aggressive bowling at the body with a legside field attracted much criticism. England won the three-Test series of three-day Tests against the Windies 2–0. The second, drawn, Test at Old Trafford, Manchester, provided an intriguing footnote to the Bodyline controversy when Manny Martindale and Learie Constantine bowled Bodyline – fast, short-pitched balls aimed at the body – against the Englishmen, the only time they faced it in international cricket. The tactic did not work, as Douglas Jardine, the English captain who ordered his players to bowl it against the Australians, did not flinch as he scored his only Test century, making 127 out of England's 374.

- **Learie Constantine**

Another England tour of the West Indies followed in 1934–35. England won the first Test in Barbados on a poor pitch, affected by rain, and in a match where 309 runs were scored, England took a four-wicket victory. Both sides declared one of their innings closed to have their bowlers take advantage of the poor pitch. The second Test saw the Windies win by 217 runs, and a drawn third Test saw the series go to a decider at Sabina Park in Jamaica. A massive 270 not out from George Headley saw the Windies declare on 535 for 7. Despite a century from Les Ames, England could not avoid going down by an innings and 161 runs – the West Indies had secured their first Test series victory.

The West Indies toured England in 1939. England won the first Test at Lord's easily by 8 wickets, then there was a rain-affected draw in Manchester, and finally a high-scoring draw at the Oval in mid-August. The highlight of the series for the West Indies was George Headley scoring hundreds in both innings in the Lord's Test. With the clouds of World War II seemingly about to envelope Europe, the rest of the tour was cancelled and the Windies returned home. They would play no more Tests until 21 January 1948 saw the start of the first Test the West Indies played since the War, which resulted in a draw against the MCC side from England. The second Test was also drawn, with George Carew and Andy Ganteaume both making centuries. Ganteaume was then dropped, ending with a Test average of 112 – the highest in Test history. The West Indies won the final two Tests chasing sub-100 totals, and wrapped up the series 2–0, their first away-series victory.

In 1948, West Indies toured newly independent India for the first time for a five Test tour. The tour was preceded by a non-Test tour of Pakistan and followed by a similar short tour of Ceylon. After three high-scoring draws against the Indians, the West Indians wrapped up the fourth by an innings before a thrilling fifth Test, which left the Indians six runs away from victory with two wickets in hand as time ran out, so that the West Indies thus won the rubber 1–0. Carrying on from his hundred in the series against England, Everton Weekes set a record of scoring hundreds in five successive Test innings.

- **The post-War period (1950s)**

1950 saw another tour of England, the series saw the emergence for the West Indies of their great spinning duo,

Sonny Ramadhin and Alf Valentine. England won the first Test by 202 runs, but Valentine and Ramadhin's bowling would win the series for the visitors. The second Test saw the Windies put on 326 thanks to 106 from Allan Rae before Valentine (4 for 48) and Ramadhin (5 for 66) skittled England in the first innings. A mammoth 168 from Clyde Walcott saw England set a theoretical target of 601. Ramadhin's 6 for 86 and Valentine's 3 for 79 dismissed the hosts for 274. The spinning duo took 12 wickets, Frank Worrell made 261 and Everton Weekes 129 as the third Test went the Windies way by 10 wickets, the fourth saw 14 wickets from Valentine and Ramadhin and centuries from Rae and Worrell as England were defeated by an innings. The West Indies won the series 3–1.

In 1951–1952 the Windies visited Australia. The first Test saw a narrow defeat by three wickets, with the two spinners seemingly continuing their form with twelve wickets between them. The second Test was lost by seven wickets, as Australia replied to the Windies 362 and 290 with 567 (which included centuries from Lindsay Hassett and Keith Miller) and 137 for 2. 6 wickets from Worrell in the third Test saw Australia dismissed for only 82, and the Windies eventually won by six wickets to pull back to two-one down in the series. The fourth Test saw the series lost in a narrow defeat. Worrell, batting with an injured hand, scored 108 and helped the Windies to 272 before Australia made 216 in reply.

203 from the Windies left Australia a target of 260. 5 wickets from Valentine helped reduced the Aussies to 222 for 9, 38 short with 1 wicket remaining. It didn't happen, as some brilliant running between the wicket for Australia by Bill Johnston and Doug Ring saw West Indies lose their composure and the match. The fifth Test saw three batting

collapses, as Australia (116 and 377) beat Windies (78 and 213) by 202 runs to finish the rubber four-one winners. The West Indies then went on to New Zealand. In the first Test encounter between the two teams, the visitors scored a five wicket victory. In the second and final Test, Allan Rae scored 99, Jeffrey Stollmeyer 152, Frank Worrell 100 and Clyde Walcott 115 as the West Indies put on 546 for 6 declared. There wasn't enough time to bowl out the opposition twice though, as the hosts made 160 and were following-on at 17 for 1 when stumps were drawn, leaving the Windies series winners.

The Indians toured at the beginning of 1953. The Windies won the second of the five Tests that were played, with the others all being draws. The highlight of these games we Frank Worrell's 237 in the fifth Test, where all the three W's scored hundreds, as the West Indies scored a 1–0 series victory. Len Hutton led an MCC (England) side to the islands in 1953–1954. Sonny Ramadhin again starred for the Windies taking 23 wickets (no other West Indian took more than 8), as Walcott's 698 runs was more than 200 higher than second-placed West Indian, Everton Weekes. The five match rubber was drawn two-all.

Australia came and conquered in 1954–1955. After the Aussies made 515 in the first innings of the first Test, the Windies went down by 9 wickets. Then the Windies 382 was put in the shade by 600 for 9 declared by the visitors as the second Test was drawn. A low-scoring third Test saw Australia (257 and 133 for 2) beat the hosts (182 and 207) by 8 wickets. After Australia scored 668 in the fourth Test, the series was lost, although a double century from captain Denis Atkinson and a world-record stand for the seventh wicket allowed the Windies to reach 510 and draw the Test. The fifth Test saw the West Indies win the toss and bat.

Walcott's 155 was the highest score of their 357.

The Australians then batted and batted, in total for 245.4 overs in the 6-day Test, as they put on 758 for 8 declared, with five players making centuries. 319 in the West Indies' second innings left them defeated by an innings and 82 runs in the Test, and by three games to nil in the series. Walcott set records by scoring five hundreds, and hundreds in both innings of a match twice. A four-Test tour of New Zealand followed in February 1956. After two wins by an innings and one by 9 wickets, the Windies were surprised by the Kiwis in the fourth, dismissing them for 145 and 77 as they recorded their first ever Test win in their 45th Test.

John Goddard returned to captain the West Indians for a five-Test tour of England in 1957, which was lost three-nil, with England having the better of the two draws. Then 1957–1958 Gerry Alexander led a team that defeated Pakistan three-one. It was in this series in Jamaica that Garry Sobers scored 365 not out to record what was then the highest score in Test match cricket. Alexander went on to lead the West Indies to a three-nil win over five Tests in India, and a 2–1 defeat by Pakistan in a three match rubber in the following winter. In 1959–1960 he led as West Indies went down one-nil at home in a five-match series with England.

- **A period of mixed fortunes (1960s)**

Despite being a region where whites are a minority, until 1960 West Indies were always captained by white cricketers, though this was more social than racial discrimination. Throughout the 1950s, social theorist CLR James, the increasingly political former cricketer Learie Constantine and others called for a black captain. Constantine himself had stood in for Jackie Grant in the field against England on the 1934–35 tour, and George Headley captained the West Indies in the First Test against England in 1947–48 when the appointed, white captain, John Goddard was injured. However, no black was appointed as captain for a whole series until Frank Worrell was chosen to lead West Indies in their tour of Australia in 1960–61. In his three years as captain, Worrell moulded a bunch of talented but raw cricketers into probably the best team in the world.

In 1960, Australia were the best team in the world but on their way down, while West Indies were on their way up. It so happened that when they met,the two teams were of almost equal strength. The result was a series that has been recognised as one of the greatest of all time. The first Test in Brisbane was the first Test ever to end in a tie, which in cricket means the side batting last has been dismissed with scores level. The teams shared the next two Tests. In the fourth, Australia's last pair of Ken Mackay and Lindsay Kline played out the last 100 minutes of the match to earn a draw, while Australia won the final Test and the series by two wickets. One of the days of play was attended by a world-record crowd of 90,800. Such was the impression created by Worrell's team that the newly instituted trophy for the series between the two teams was named the Frank Worrell Trophy.

West Indies beat India 5–0 at home next year, and in 1963, they beat a fine English team by three matches to one. The Lord's Test of this series saw a famous finish. With two balls left, England needed six runs to win, and West Indies one wicket. The non-striker was Colin Cowdrey, who had his left arm in a sling, having fractured it earlier in the day. However, David Allen safely played out the last two balls and the match ended in a draw. Worrell retired at the end of the series. The selectors picked Garry Sobers to succeed him.

Worrell did, however, serve as the team manager when West Indies hosted Australia in 1964–65. The matches against Australia were bitterly fought, with accusations about Charlie Griffith's action and bouncer wars. The West Indies won this series 2–1 to be the unofficial world champions. Sobers was not as good at man-management as Worrell and cracks soon began to appear. Often it was his individual brilliance that made the difference between a win and a loss. Throughout the 1960s, West Indies bowling was led by Wes Hall, Griffith, Lance Gibbs and Sobers himself. Hall and Griffith faded and then retired by the end of the decade, but WI could find no replacement for them till the mid-1970s.

Sobers was at his best in England in 1966, scoring 722 runs and taking 20 wickets in the five Tests. Three times he topped 150, and the 163* at Lord's turned a certain defeat into a near victory. West Indies won 3–1. England toured the West Indies in 1967–68 for a series that became noted for England's deliberate slow play. West Indies were forced to follow on in the first Test but saved it without difficulty. The second Test was played on an underprepared wicket at Kingston. England won an important toss and scored 376. The bounce of the wicket having become very uneven, West Indies collapsed to 143 and followed on. On the fourth day in the second innings, a disputed decision led to a crowd riot, and the match had to be stopped for some time.

In a curious decision, the West Indian Cricket Board (WICB) agreed to add a 75-minute sixth day to compensate for the lost time. Sobers played an outstanding innings of 113 not out, which allowed West Indies to set England a target of 159 in 155 minutes. England just about saved the game, losing eight wickets for 68. In the fourth Test West Indies gained a first innings lead of 122 at Port-of-Spain, but with the second innings score at 92 for 2, Sobers, frustrated by England's slow over rates and wanting to give himself a chance, albeit a small one, to win, surprisingly declared the innings, a decision for which he was widely criticised at the time. England were set a target of 215 in 165 minutes and they achieved it with 3 minutes to spare. West Indies made one last effort to win the final Test, but England drew it with only wicket left in their second innings. West Indies lost the series 0–1, the first defeat since 1960–61.

Australia and Bill Lawry had their revenge in 1968–69, when West Indies lost the away series 1–3. New Zealand managed to draw the series that followed, and then in 1969 West Indies were defeated 0–2 in England.

- **World dominance (1970s)**

West Indies' woes overflowed into the 1970s. At home in 1970–71, they lost to India for the first time. In the next year, a five Test series against New Zealand cricket team ended with no team coming close to winning one. A major find in the New Zealand series was Lawrence Rowe, who started off with a double century and century on his debut. Under Rohan Kanhai's captaincy, West Indies showed the first signs of revival. Australia won the closely fought 1972–73 series in the Caribbean by two Tests. With Sobers back – but Kanhai still the captain – West Indies defeated England 2–0 in 1973. This included a win by an innings and 226 runs at Lord's, their biggest win against England. The return series in West Indies ended 1–1, though the home team was the better side. Rowe continued his run scoring three centuries including a 302 at Kingston. The final Test of this 1973–74 series marked the end of an era in West Indies cricket – it was the last Test of both Garry Sobers and Rohan Kanhai, and marked the emergence of fast bowler Andy Roberts.

The new captain Clive Lloyd had made his first appearance in Test cricket in 1966 and had since become a fixture in the side. His avuncular, bespectacled appearance and a stoop near the shoulders masked the fact that he was a very fine fielder, especially in the covers, and a devastating stroke player. Lloyd's first assignment was the tour of India in 1974–75. West Indies won the first two Tests comfortably. Gordon Greenidge started his career with 107 and 93 in the first Test. Vivian Richards failed on his debut, but scored 192* in his second. India fought back to win the next two, but Lloyd hit 242* in the final Test to win the series.

- **Flag of the West Indies cricket team prior to 1999**

West Indies won the inaugural World Cup in England in 1975, defeating Australia in the final. Then in 1975–76 they toured Australia, only to lose 1–5 in the six-Test series, and then beat India at home two-one in a four Test series later that same winter. It was in Australia that the quick bowler Michael Holding made his first appearance. Colin Croft and Joel Garner made their debuts the next year, and Malcolm Marshall two years after. In the span of about four years, West Indies brought together a bowling line-up of a quality that had rarely been seen before. The tour of India had seen the debut of Vivian Richards, arguably the finest West Indian batsman ever, and Gordon Greenidge, who joined a strong batting line-up that already included Alvin Kallicharran and opener Roy Fredericks in addition to Rowe and Lloyd. These players formed the nucleus of the side that became recognised as world Test match champions until the beginning of the 1990s.

Next came a tour of England in 1976. In a TV interview before the series, English captain Tony Greig commented that the West Indies tend to do badly under pressure and that "we'll make them grovel". This comment, especially as it came from a South African-born player, touched a raw nerve of the West Indians. Throughout the series, the English batsmen were subjected to what was described by the English press as very hostile bowling, but was rather reflective of a solid pace attack, and what the Windies had faced in Australia before. After the first two Tests ended in draws, West Indies won the next three. Of the many heroes for West Indies, Richards stood out with 829 runs in four Tests. He hit 232 at Trent Bridge and 291 at the Oval. Greenidge scored three hundreds, two of which were on the difficult wicket at Old Trafford. Roberts and Holding shared 55 wickets between them, Holding's 8 for 92 and 6 for 57 on the unhelpful wicket at the Oval being a superlative effort.

West Indies won a home series against a tough Pakistan side in 1976–77. A few months later, the World Series Cricket (WSC) controversy broke out. Most of the West Indian players signed up with Kerry Packer, an Australian TV magnate who was attempting to set up his own international cricket competition. The Australian team that toured West Indies the next year included no Packer players. West Indies Cricket Board fielded a full-strength team under the argument that none of the West Indies players had refused to play, but disputes arose in the matter of payment and about the selection of certain players. Before the third Test, Lloyd resigned his captaincy. Within two days all the other WSC-contracted players also withdrew. Alvin Kallicharran captained the team for the remaining Tests of the series, which the Windies won 3–1.

WICB allowed the WSC players to appear in the 1979 World Cup, and the West Indies retained the title with little difficulty. By the end of 1979, the WSC disputes were resolved. Kallicharran was deposed after losing a six-match series one-nil in India and Lloyd returned as captain for a tour against a full-strength Australia (where the Windies won two-nil, with one draw) and New Zealand. The latter tour was full of controversy.

New Zealand won the first Test at Dunedin by one wicket, but West Indies were never happy with the umpiring. West Indian discontent boiled over the next Test at Christchurch. While running into bowl, Colin Croft deliberately shouldered the umpire Fred Goodall. When Goodall went to talk to Lloyd about Croft's behaviour, he had to walk all the way to meet the West Indian captain, as the latter did not move an inch from his position at the slips. After tea on the third day, West Indies refused to take the field unless Goodall was removed. They were persuaded to continue, and it took intense negotiations between the two boards to keep the tour on track. The Kiwis won the three match series after the second and third Tests ended in draws. Nevertheless, the defeat proved to be the West Indies last Test series loss for the next 15 years.

After losing their first series of the 1980s in March 1980, the West Indies went throughout the rest of the decade undefeated.

The 1980s started with a one-nil victory away to England over five Tests, one-nil away to Pakistan over four Tests, two-nil home to England over four Tests and a one-all draw away to Australia. Then in 1982–83, a West Indian rebel team toured apartheid South Africa. It was led by Lawrence Rowe and included prominent players like Alvin

Kallicharran, Colin Croft, Collis King and Sylvester Clarke. WICB banned the players for life (which was later revoked), and some were refused entry back home. However, the rebels managed another tour the next year, which included most of the players of the original team.

Despite this loss of talent, the official Windies side continued to dominate. During this time, the West Indies established themselves as one of Test cricket's all-time great sides, peaking perhaps on their tour of England in 1984, where they won the series 5–0, the only time in Test cricket history the touring side has whitewashed a five-test series. This was followed by a second "blackwash" against England at home in 1985–86. At the same time, the West Indies established the then-record of 11 consecutive Test victories, which was part of a still-standing record of 27 Tests without defeat. In the period from 1980 to 1985–86 they won 10 out of 11 Test series, the 1981–82 series in Australia being drawn 1–1. The West Indies' only notable defeat in this period was in the one-day arena, when, to general surprise, they lost to India in the final of the 1983 World Cup.

West Indian captain Lloyd retired from Test cricket at the end of the 1984–85 series against Australia. In total Lloyd had captained West Indies in 74 Test matches, winning 36 of them. Vivian Richards was Lloyd's successor, and continued the run of success. Meanwhile, a change of old guard was also happening. Joel Garner and Michael Holding had retired by 1987. A major find was Curtly Ambrose, who was as tall as Garner and equally effective with the ball.

Courtney Walsh, who made his first appearance in 1984, bowled with an action that resembled Holding. Ian Bishop also had a similar action, and was as good a bowler till injuries interrupted his career. Patrick Patterson was faster than all the rest, but had a short career. Marshall still was the finest fast bowler in the world. But the batting was beginning to show signs of weakness, despite the presence of Richards, Greenidge and Desmond Haynes. West Indies failed to qualify for the semifinals of the 1987 World Cup. By the end of the 1980s, while still good were very beatable, they had lost the aura of invincibility that they had till the middle of the decade. Finding good replacements for senior players was again becoming a problem.

- **Fall from grace (1990s–2000s)**

During the early 1990s, the West Indies team was dealt a great blow with the retirement of its star players like Richards, Greenidge, Dujon and Marshall (who all retired after the away series against England in 1991), bringing an end of an era of strength. This left a youthful and inexperienced side. After Richards‘ retirement the only players with significant experience were Richie Richardson (who was appointed the new captain of the side), Desmond Haynes (who was soon dropped), Gus Logie (who was recalled), Courtney Walsh (who was now the leader of the West Indian pace attack) and Roger Harper (who came and went).

However, this did not immediately affect their performance. Richie Richardson proved to be a decent successor to Richards. A new crop of young players emerged such as Brian Lara, Curtly Ambrose, Ian Bishop, Jimmy Adams, Carl Hooper, Phil Simmons, Keith Arthurton and Winston Benjamin. It was five more years before the West Indies lost a series, but they had a number of close shaves before then. Making a comeback to international cricket, South Africa played its first Test match in

Bridgetown, a match which was attended by fewer than 10,000 people because of a boycott. Needing 201 to win on the last day, South Africa reached 123 for 2 before Ambrose and Walsh took the remaining 8 wickets for 25 runs. In 1992–93, the West Indies defeated Australia by one run in Adelaide, where a loss would have cost them the series. In 1994–95, the West Indies salvaged a draw in India when, after losing the first Test and drawing the second, they secured a win in the third. In 1992, the West Indies once again failed to qualify for the World Cup semi-finals.

Australia finally defeated the West Indies 2–1 in 1994–95 to become the unofficial world champions of Test cricket. The 1996 World Cup ended with a defeat in the semi-final, which forced Richie Richardson to end his career. The captaincy passed over to Courtney Walsh and then in 1998 to Brian Lara. The West Indies made their first ever official tour to South Africa in 1998–99. It was a disaster, starting with player revolts and ending with a 5–0 defeat. The 1999 World Cup campaign ended in the group stages. The next year, England won a series against the West Indies for the first time in thirty-one years. The West Indies ended the decade with another 5–0 defeat, this time in Australia.

For most of the 1990s, the West Indian batting lineup was dominated by Brian Lara. Lara became a regular in the side after the retirement of Viv Richards in 1991. In 1993–94, he scored 375 against England in Antigua, breaking Sobers' world record for the highest individual score in Test cricket. He continued his fine form playing for Warwickshire in the 1994 English County Championship, posting seven first-class hundreds in eight innings (including the Test match 375). The last of these was 501 not out against Durham, which improved upon Hanif Mohammad's thirty-five-year-old record as the highest score in first-class cricket. The

West Indian bowling attack was spearheaded by Curtly Ambrose and Courtney Walsh, the latter setting a then world record of 519 wickets. However, these two had both retired by 2001, and their successors failed to maintain the high standards that Ambrose and Walsh had set. Despite the emergence of some good batsmen like Shivnarine Chanderpaul and Ramnaresh Sarwan, Brian Lara remained the crucial figure of the side.

After a 2–0 defeat by New Zealand in 1999–00, Lara was replaced as captain by Jimmy Adams, who initially enjoyed series wins against Zimbabwe and Pakistan. However, a 3–1 defeat by England and a 5–0 whitewash by Australia saw him replaced by Carl Hooper for the 2000–01 visit by South Africa. By the time Lara was restored to the captaincy in 2002–03, series had been lost to South Africa, Sri Lanka, Pakistan, New Zealand and India. The only series win of note was against India (although Zimbabwe and Bangladesh were also beaten) as the West Indies plummeted to eighth place in the world-rankings, below all the other established Test nations.

After losing the first series of his second captaincy period to world champions Australia, Lara secured success against Sri Lanka and Zimbabwe, before another poor run saw 3–0 defeats in 4-Test series against both South Africa and England. In the drawn fourth Test against England, Lara became the only man to regain the world record for highest individual Test score by scoring 400 not out, once again in Antigua, bettering Matthew Hayden's 380 against Zimbabwe the previous year. The West Indies were then whitewashed 4–0 in England. Lara's last act as captain was to win the 2004 ICC Champions Trophy, a one-day competition second only to the Cricket World Cup, at the Oval, London – a win that was a welcome surprise for the

Caribbean which had just been hit by Hurricane Ivan.

- **Player, Board disputes**

This joy was short-lived as a major dispute broke out in 2005 between the West Indian Players Association (WIPA) and the Cricket Board. The point of contention was clause 5 of the tour contract which gave WICB the sole and exclusive right to arrange for sponsorship, advertising, licensing, merchandising and promotional activities relating to WICB or any WICB Team. Digicel were the sponsors of the West Indian Team, while most of the players had contracts with Cable & Wireless.

This conflict, coupled with a payment dispute meant that the West Indies initially announced a team absent Lara and a number of other leading West Indians for South Africa's visit in 2004–05, leading to Shivnarine Chanderpaul becoming captain. Some of these players did, in the end, compete. However, the dispute had not been resolved and rumbled on, leading to a second-string side being named for the tour of Sri Lanka in 2005. A resolution did not arise until October 2005, when a full-strength side was finally named for the 2005–06 tour of Australia. It was on this tour that Brian Lara overtook Australian Allan Border as the highest run-scorer in Test match cricket, despite the West Indies losing the series 3–0.

In 2009, another dispute erupted when many senior players decided not to take part over pay and contract issues. The WICB chose a second-string side to take part in a series against Bangladesh and the Champions Trophy. In 2012, ICC decided to get involved in order to resolve this long standing dispute.

In 2014, another dispute between WICB and West Indian Players Association (WIPA) led to the team's Indian tour being curtailed. The bone of contention was a protracted payment structure.

In 2015, Players has made themselves unavailable for tests, and with Jason Holder being thrust into the role of captaincy, and was met with much distrust between veteran bowlers and Holder and the administration and selectors. As a result, West Indies lost 21 matches by an innings since 1995–2015, when the team never lost more than 4 matches by over an innings combined from 1966 to 1995.

- **Rebuilding and T20 success (2010s)**

When Twenty20 cricket began to be contested full force beginning with the 2007 World Twenty20 in South Africa, the West Indies began to develop and realize an advantage of possessing and developing Richards-style batsmen who could devastate bowling attacks with power. As well, many West Indian batsmen put an emphasis on power to prepare for Twenty20 play as it offered them their most lucrative contracts. Foremost among the hard hitters was Chris Gayle, who both hit the first T20 international century and became the first to hit two.

At the 2012 World Twenty20 in Sri Lanka, the West Indies beat Australia in the semifinals and then beat the hosts by 32 runs to win their third ICC world championship and their first since Richards, Holding. and Lloyd had won the 1979 World Cup. In the 2016 World Twenty20, they beat host India in the semifinals after a successful chase and were still cheered back at their hotel by local and traveling fans as they advanced to face England in the final, which they won by four wickets after Carlos Brathwaite hit four consecutive sixes off Ben Stokes with 19 runs required off the final over. In contrast to being 8th in the ICC Test Rankings and 9th in the ICC ODI Rankings, the West Indies entered the match as second in the ICC T20 rankings behind India.

- **West Indies cricket team**

The West Indies cricket team, nicknamed the Windies, is a multi-national men's cricket team representing the mainly English-speaking countries and territories in the Caribbean region and administered by Cricket West Indies. The players on this composite team are selected from a chain of fifteen Caribbean nation-states and territories. As of 26 November 2022, the West Indies cricket team is ranked eighth in Tests, and tenth in ODIs and seventh in T20Is in the official ICC rankings.

From the mid-late 1970s to the early 1990s, the West Indies team was the strongest in the world in both Test and One Day International cricket. A number of cricketers who were considered among the best in the world have hailed from the West Indies: Garfield Sobers, Lance Gibbs, George Headley, Brian Lara, Vivian Richards, Clive Lloyd, Malcolm Marshall, Alvin Kallicharran, Andy Roberts, Rohan Kanhai, Frank Worrell, Clyde Walcott, Everton Weekes, Curtly Ambrose, Michael Holding, Courtney Walsh, Joel Garner, and Wes Hall have all been inducted into the ICC Cricket Hall of Fame.

The West Indies have won the ICC Cricket World Cup twice (1975 and 1979, when it was styled the Prudential Cup), the ICC T20 World Cup twice (2012 and 2016, when it was styled World Twenty20), the ICC Champions Trophy once

(2004), the ICC Under 19 Cricket World Cup once (2016), and have also finished as runners-up in the Cricket World Cup (1983), the Under 19 Cricket World Cup (2004), and the ICC Champions Trophy (2006). The West Indies appeared in three consecutive World Cup finals (1975, 1979 and 1983), and were the first team to win back-to-back World Cups (1975 and 1979), both of these records have been surpassed only by Australia, who appeared in 4 consecutive World Cup Finals (1996, 1999, 2003 and 2007) winning 3 consecutive World Cups (1999, 2003 and 2007).

- **History of the West Indian cricket team**

Learie Constantine, who played Test cricket in the 1920s and 1930s, was one of the first great West Indian players.Darren Sammy. The West Indies have won three major tournament titles: the Champions Trophy once, and the World Twenty20 twice. Both World T20s were won with Sammy as captain, making him the only West Indian captain besides Clive Lloyd with multiple ICC tournament victories.

The history of the West Indies cricket team began in the 1890s, when the first representative sides were selected to play visiting English sides. The WICB joined the sport's international ruling body, the Imperial Cricket Conference, in 1926, and played their first official international match, granted Test status, in 1928, thus becoming the fourth Test 'nation'. In their early days in the 1930s, the side represented the British colonies that would later form the West Indies Federation plus British Guiana.

The last series the West Indies played before the outbreak of the Second World War was against England in 1939. There followed a hiatus that lasted until January 1948 when the MCC toured the West Indies. Of the West Indies players in that first match after the war only Gerry Gomez, George Headley, Jeffrey Stollmeyer, and Foffie Williams had previously played Test cricket. In 1948, leg spinner Wilfred Ferguson became the first West Indian bowler to take ten wickets in a Test, finishing with 11/229 in a match against England; later that same year Hines Johnson became the first West Indies fast bowler to achieve the feat, managing 10/96 against the same opponents.

The West Indies defeated England for the first time at Lord's on 29 June 1950. Ramadhin and Alf Valentine were the architects of the victory which inspired a calypso by Lord Beginner. Later on 16 August 1950, completed a 3–1 series win when they won at The Oval. Although blessed with some great players in their early days as a Test team, their successes remained sporadic until the 1960s when the side changed from a white-dominated to a black-dominated side under the successive captaincies of Frank Worrell and Gary Sobers.

By the late 1970s, the West Indies led by Clive Lloyd had a side recognised as unofficial world champions, a reputation they retained throughout the 1980s. During these glory years, the West Indies were noted for their four-man fast bowling attack, backed up by some of the best batsmen in the world. In 1976, fast bowler Michael Holding took 14/149 in the OvalTest against England, setting a record which still stands for best bowling figures in a Test by a West Indies bowler. The 1980s saw the team set a then-record streak of 11 consecutive Test victories in 1984 and inflict two 5–0 "blackwashes" on England.

Throughout the 1990s and 2000s, however, West Indian cricket declined, largely owing to the failure of the West Indian Cricket Board to move the game from an amateur pastime to a professional sport, coupled with the general economic decline in West Indian countries, and the team struggling to retain its past glory. Victory in the 2004 Champions Trophy and a runner-up showing in the 2006 Champions Trophy left some hopeful, but it was not until the inception of Twenty20 cricket that the West Indies began to regain a place among the cricketing elite and among cricket fans, as they developed ranks of players capable of taking over games with their power hitting, including Chris Gayle, Kieron Pollard, Marlon Samuels, Lendl Simmons, DJ Bravo, Andre Russell and Carlos Brathwaite.

They beat Australia and then host Sri Lanka in the 2012 World Twenty20 to win their first ICC world championship since the 1979 World Cup and then bested England to win the 2016 World Twenty20, making them the first team to win the World Twenty20 twice. As an added bonus, the West Indies also became the first to win both the men's and women's World Twenty20 on the same day, as the women's team beat three-time defending champion Australia for their first ICC world title immediately beforehand.

- **Flag and anthem**

Former flag of the West Indies cricket team used until 1999. This flag became public domain but the current version is copyrighted.Most cricketing nations use their own national flags for cricketing purposes. However, as the West Indies represent a number of independent states and dependencies, there is no natural choice of flag. The WICB has, therefore, developed an insignia showing a palm tree and cricket stumps on a small sunny island.

The insignia, on a maroon background, makes up the West Indian flag. The background sometimes has a white stripe above a green stripe, which is separated by a maroon stripe, passing horizontally through the middle of the background. Prior to 1999, the WICB(C) had used a similar insignia featuring a cabbage palm tree and an island, but there were no stumps and, instead of the sun, there was the constellation Orion. It was designed in 1923 by Sir Algernon Aspinall, then Secretary of the West India Committee. Around the same time in the 1920s the suggested motto for the West Indies team was "Nec curat Orion leones", which comes from a quote by Horace, meaning that Orion, as symbolical of the West Indies XI, does not worry about the lions.For ICC tournaments, "Rally 'Round the West Indies" by David Rudder is used as the team's anthem.

- **List of cricket grounds in the West Indies**

The following eleven stadiums have been used for at least one Test match. The number of Tests played at each venue followed by the number of One Day Internationals and twenty20 internationals played at that venue is in brackets as of 2 April 2021.

Queen's Park Oval – Port of Spain, Trinidad (61/73/6): The Queen's Park Oval has hosted more Test matches than any other ground in the Caribbean and first hosted a Test match in 1930. The ground is considered one of the most picturesque venues in the world of cricket, featuring the view Trinidad's Northern Range. It has a capacity of over 18,000.

Kensington Oval – Bridgetown, Barbados (55/44/23):Kensington Oval hosted the region's first Test match in 1930 and is recognised as the 'Mecca' of West Indies cricket.

Its capacity was increased from 15,000 to 28,000 for the 2007 World Cup and down to its current capacity of 11,000 post – World Cup. It has hosted two ICC world finals – the 2007 Cricket World Cup Final, which Australia won over Sri Lanka, and the 2010 World Twenty20 Final, which England won against Australia.

Bourda – Georgetown, Guyana (30/11/0): Bourda first hosted a Test match in 1930. It was the only Test ground in South America (until the use of Providence), and the only one below sea level and with its own moat (to prevent the pitch from frequent flooding). It has a capacity of around 22,000. It is remembered for the Pitch Invasion during an April 1999, One Day International between Australia and the West Indies, with Australia needing 3 runs to tie and 4 to win off the last ball, a full scale pitch invasion, resulted in the match being deemed a tie, due to the stumps having been stolen before the West Indian team could effect a run out.

Sabina Park – Kingston, Jamaica (54/41/6): Sabina Park first hosted a Test match in 1930. The Blue Mountains, which are famed for their coffee, form the backdrop. Sabina Park played host to Garry Sobers' then world-record 365 not out. In 1998, the Test against England was abandoned here on the opening day because the pitch was too dangerous. It has a capacity of 15,000.

Antigua Recreation Ground – St John's, Antigua (22/11/0): Antigua Recreation Ground first hosted a Test in 1981. Three Test triple centuries have been scored on this ground: Chris Gayle's 317 in 2005, and Brian Lara's world record scores of 375 in 1994 and 400 not out in 2004. The historic stadium was removed from the roster of grounds hosting international matches in June 2006, to make way for the island's new cricket stadium, being constructed 3 miles outside the capital city expected to be completed in time for its hosting of matches for Cricket World Cup 2007. However, after the abandoned Test match between England and the West Indies in February 2009 at the new North Sound ground, Test cricket returned to the ARG.

Darren Sammy National Cricket Stadium – Gros Islet, St Lucia (10/26/17): Originally the Beauséjour Cricket Ground, first hosted a Test in 2003. It has a capacity of 12,000. This was the first stadium in the Caribbean to host a day-night cricket match. The match was between the West Indies and Zimbabwe. New Zealand was scheduled to play a test in 2014 to mark the return to Test cricket after a break of 8 years. Following the West Indies' victory in the 2016 World Twenty20, the St. Lucian government renamed the venue after captain Sammy, a native St. Lucian, with another St. Lucian – Johnson Charles – having a stand named in his honor after also being part of the 2012 and 2016 championship squads.

Warner Park Stadium – Basseterre, St Kitts (3/18/10): The Warner Park Sporting Complex hosted its first One Day International on 23 May 2006 and its first Test match on 22 June 2006. The stadium has a permanent capacity of 8,000, with provisions for temporary stands to enable the hosting figure to past 10,000.

Providence Stadium – Georgetown, Guyana (2/24/8): The Providence Stadium hosted its first One Day International on 28 March 2007 for the 2007 Cricket World Cup and its first Test match on 22 March 2008. The stadium has a permanent capacity of 15,000, and is to host Test cricket instead of Bourda.

Sir Vivian Richards Stadium – North Sound, Antigua (12/ 20/4): The Sir Viv Richards Stadium hosted its first One Day International on 27 March 2007 for the 2007 Cricket World

Cup and its first Test match on 30 May 2008. The stadium has a permanent capacity of 10,000, and is to host Test cricket instead of the Antigua Recreation Ground.

Windsor Park Stadium – Roseau, Dominica (5/4/4): Windsor Park is another home venue for the West Indian team. Construction first started on it in 2005, and it finally opened in October 2007, too late to serve as a venue for the 2007 Cricket World Cup. It hosts first-class cricket and hosted its first test on 6 July 2011 against India, however it held its first One Day International on 26 July 2009. It has a seating capacity of 12,000.

Three further stadia have been used for One Day Internationals, or Twenty20 Internationals but not Test matches. The number of One Day Internationals and Twenty20 Internationals played at each venue is shown in the table below:

- **Clothing**

Viv Richards, who has a Test batting average of 50.23 from 121 matches, captained the West Indies from 1985–86 to 1991, a period throughout which the West Indies were the best Test match side in the world.When playing one-day cricket, the Windies wear a maroon-coloured shirt and trousers. The shirt also sports the logo of the West Indian Cricket Board and the name of their suppliers Castore on the sleeves of their jerseys. The one-day cap is maroon with the WICB logo on the left of the front, with two yellow stripes.

When playing first-class cricket, in addition to their cricket flannels West Indian fielders sometimes wear a maroon sunhat with a wide brim or a maroon baggy cap. The WICB logo is on the front of the hat. Helmets are coloured similarly. The sweater was edged with Maroon, green and grey. Gold was added to the stripes in the early 2000s. The design reverted to a simple maroon facing when the West Indies began wearing fleeces. In 2020 they again wore the traditional cable knit sweaters edged with Maroon and Green. When the team toured they wore maroon caps but in test matches in the Caribbean, it was customary for the team to wear dark blue caps until the late 1970s. The blazers awarded for home tests were dark blue with white and green facings. An example is displayed in the museum at Lord's. After c 1977 home and away teams both wore maroon caps and the blazers were the same colours.

During World Series Cricket, coloured uniforms were adopted. The initial West Indies uniform was pink and was later changed to maroon to match their Test match caps. Grey was also added as a secondary colour. In some of their uniforms grey has been dominant over the traditional maroon. Some uniforms had green, yellow or white as accent colour.

Former uniform suppliers were and BLK (2017-2019), Joma (2015-2017) Woodworm (2008-2015), Admiral (2000-2005), Asics (1999 World Cup), UK Sportsgear (1997-1998), ISC (1992-1996) and Adidas (1979-1991).

- **West Indies women's cricket team**

The West Indies women's cricket team enjoy a much lower profile than the men's team. They played 11 Test matches between 1975–76 and 1979, winning once, losing three times, and drawing the other games. Since then, they have only played one further Test match, a draw game against Pakistan in 2003–04.

They also have an infrequent record in One Day Internationals. A team from Trinidad and Tobago and a team from Jamaica played in the first women's World Cup in 1973, with both sides faring poorly, finishing fifth and sixth respectively out of a field of seven. The Windies united as a team to play their first ODI in 1979, but thereafter did not play until the 1993 World Cup. The side has never been one of the leading sides in the world, however, since the 2013 World Cup, where the team finished runner-ups, the team has improved reasonably well. Their main success being achieving second place in the International Women's Cricket Council Trophy, a competition for the second tier of women's national cricket teams, in 2003. Their overall record in one-dayers is to have played 177, won 80, lost 91 with one tie and 5 no results .

Because of the women's side's relatively low profile, there are few well-known names in the game. The most notable is probably Nadine George, a wicket-keeper/ batsman, who became the first, and to date only, West Indian woman to score a Test century, in Karachi, Pakistan in 2003–04. George is a prominent supporter of sport in the West Indies, and in particular, in her native St Lucia, and in 2005 was made an MBE by the Prince of Wales for services to sport.

2016 saw the West Indies women win their first ICC world championship – the 2016 Women's World Twenty20, after beating three-time defending champion Australia by eight wickets at Eden Gardens with members of the men's team in the crowd to support.

THREE

HISTORY OF CRICKET

- **History of cricket**

The sport of cricket has a known history beginning in the late 16th century. Having originated in south-east England, it became an established sport in the country in the 18th century and developed globally in the 19th and 20th centuries. International matches have been played since the 19th-century and formal Test cricket matches are considered to date from 1877. Cricket is the world's second most popular spectator sport after association football (soccer).

Internationally, cricket is governed by the International Cricket Council (ICC) which has over one hundred countries and territories in membership although only twelve currently play Test cricket.

- **Origin**

Cricket was probably created during Saxon or Norman times by children living in the Weald, an area of dense woodlands and clearings in south-east England that lies across Kent and Sussex. The first definite written reference is from the end of the 16th-century.

There have been several speculations about the game's origins, including some that it was created in France or Flanders. The earliest of these speculative references is from 1300 and concerns the future King Edward II playing at "creag and other games" in both Westminster and Newenden. It has been suggested that "creag" was an Old English word for cricket, but expert opinion is that it was an early spelling of "craic", meaning "fun and games in general".

It is generally believed that cricket survived as a children's game for many generations before it was increasingly taken up by adults around the beginning of the 17th century. Possibly cricket was derived from bowls, assuming bowls is the older sport, by the intervention of a batsman trying to stop the ball from reaching its target by hitting it away. Playing on sheep-grazed land or in clearings, the original implements may have been a matted lump of sheep's wool (or even a stone or a small lump of wood) as the ball; a stick or a crook or another farm tool as the bat; and a stool or a tree stump or a gate (e.g., a wicket gate) as the wicket.

- **First definite reference**

John Derrick was a pupil at the Royal Grammar School, then the Free School, in Guildford when he and his friends played creckett circa 1550.

In 1597 (Old Style – 1598 New Style) a court case in England concerning an ownership dispute over a plot of common land in Guildford, Surrey, mentions the game of creckett. A 59-year-old coroner, John Derrick, testified that he and his school friends had played creckett on the site fifty years earlier when they attended the Free School. Derrick's account proves beyond reasonable doubt that the game was being played in Surrey circa 1550, and is the earliest universally accepted reference to the game.

The first reference to cricket being played as an adult sport was in 1611, when two men in Sussex were prosecuted for playing cricket on Sunday instead of going to church. In the same year, a dictionary defined cricket as a boys‘ game, and this suggests that adult participation was a recent development.

- **Derivation of the name of "cricket"**

A number of words are thought to be possible sources for the term "cricket". In the earliest definite reference, it was spelled creckett. The name may have been derived from the Middle Dutch krick(-e), meaning a stick; or the Old English cricc or cryce meaning a crutch or staff, or the French word criquet meaning a wooden post. The Middle Dutch word krickstoel means a long low stool used for kneeling in church; this resembled the long low wicket with two stumps used in early cricket. According to Heiner Gillmeister, a European language expert of the University of Bonn, "cricket" derives from the Middle Dutch phrase for hockey, met de (krik ket)sen (i.e., "with the stick chase").

It is more likely that the terminology of cricket was based on words in use in south-east England at the time and, given trade connections with the County of Flanders, especially in the 15th century when it belonged to the Duchy of Burgundy, many Middle Dutch words found their way into southern English dialects.

- **The Commonwealth**

After the Civil War ended in 1648, the new Puritan government clamped down on "unlawful assemblies", in particular the more raucous sports such as football. Their laws also demanded a stricter observance of the Sabbath than there had been previously. As the Sabbath was the only free time available to the lower classes, cricket's popularity may have waned during the Commonwealth. However, it did flourish in public fee-paying schools such as Winchester and St Paul's. There is no actual evidence that Oliver Cromwell's regime banned cricket specifically and there are references to it during the interregnum that suggest it was acceptable to the authorities provided that it did not cause any "breach of the Sabbath". It is believed that the nobility in general adopted cricket at this time through involvement in village games.

- **Gambling and press coverage**

Cricket thrived after the Restoration in 1660 and is believed to have first attracted gamblers making large bets at this time. It is possible, as believed by some historians, that top-class matches began. In 1664, the "Cavalier" Parliament passed the Gaming Act 1664 which limited stakes to £100, although that was still a fortune at the time, equivalent to about £16,000 in present-day terms. Cricket had become a significant gambling sport by the end of the 17th century, as evidenced in 1697 by a newspaper report of a "great match" played in Sussex which was 11-a-side and played for high stakes of 50 guineas a side.

With freedom of the press having been granted in 1696, cricket for the first time could be reported in the newspapers. But it was a long time before the newspaper industry adapted sufficiently to provide frequent, let alone comprehensive, coverage of the game. During the first half of the 18th century, press reports tended to focus on the betting rather than on the play.

- **18th-century cricket**

Gambling introduced the first patrons because some of the gamblers decided to strengthen their bets by forming their own teams and it is believed the first "county teams" were formed in the aftermath of the Restoration in 1660, especially as members of the nobility were employing "local experts" from village cricket as the earliest professionals. The first known game in which the teams use county names is in 1709 but there can be little doubt that these sort of fixtures were being arranged long before that. The match in 1697 was probably Sussex versus another county.

The most notable of the early patrons were a group of aristocrats and businessmen who were active from about 1725, which is the time that press coverage became more regular, perhaps as a result of the patrons' influence. These men included the 2nd Duke of Richmond, Sir William Gage, Alan Brodrick and Edwin Stead. For the first time, the press mentions individual players like Thomas Waymark.

- **Cricket expands beyond England**

Cricket was introduced to North America via the English colonies in the 17th century, probably before it had even reached the north of England. In the 18th century it arrived in other parts of the globe. It was introduced to the West Indies by colonists and to India by East India Company mariners in the first half of the century. It arrived in Australia almost as soon as colonisation began in 1788. New Zealand and South Africa followed in the early years of the 19th century.

Cricket never caught on in Canada, despite efforts by the upper class to promote the game as a way of identifying with the "mother country". Canada, unlike Australia and the West Indies, witnessed a continual decline in the popularity of the game during 1860 to 1960. Linked in the public consciousness to an upper-class sport, the game never became popular with the general public. In the summer season it had to compete with baseball. During the First World War, Canadian units stationed in France played baseball instead of cricket.

- **Development Laws of Cricket**

It's not clear when the basic rules of cricket such as bat and ball, the wicket, pitch dimensions, overs, how out, etc. were originally formulated. In 1728, the Duke of Richmond and Alan Brodick drew up Articles of Agreement to determine the code of practice in a particular game and this became a common feature, especially around payment of stake money and distributing the winnings given the importance of gambling.

In 1744, the Laws of Cricket were codified for the first time and then amended in 1774, when innovations such as lbw, middle stump and maximum bat width were added.

These laws stated that "the principals shall choose from amongst the gentlemen present two umpires who shall absolutely decide all disputes". The codes were drawn up by the so-called "Star and Garter Club" whose members ultimately founded the Marylebone Cricket Club at Lord's in 1787. The MCC immediately became the custodian of the Laws and has made periodic revisions and recodifications subsequently.

- **Continued growth in England**

The game continued to spread throughout England, and, in 1751, Yorkshire is first mentioned as a venue. The original form of bowling (i.e., rolling the ball along the ground as in bowls) was superseded sometime after 1760 when bowlers began to pitch the ball and study variations in line, length and pace. Scorecards began to be kept on a regular basis from 1772; since then, an increasingly clear picture has emerged of the sport's development.

- **An artwork depicting the history of the cricket bat**

The first famous clubs were London and Dartford in the early 18th century. London played its matches on the Artillery Ground, which still exists. Others followed, particularly Slindon in Sussex, which was backed by the Duke of Richmond and featured the star player Richard Newland. There were other prominent clubs at Maidenhead, Hornchurch, Maidstone, Sevenoaks, Bromley, Addington, Hadlow and Chertsey.

But far and away the most famous of the early clubs was Hambledon in Hampshire. It started as a parish organisation that first achieved prominence in 1756. The club itself was founded in the 1760s and was well patronised to the extent that it was the focal point of the game for about thirty years until the formation of MCC and the opening of Lord's Cricket Ground in 1787. Hambledon produced several outstanding players including the master batsman John Small and the first great fast bowler Thomas Brett. Their most notable opponent was the Chertsey and Surrey bowler Edward "Lumpy" Stevens, who is believed to have been the main proponent of the flighted delivery.

It was in answer to the flighted, or pitched, delivery that the straight bat was introduced. The old "hockey stick"–style of bat was only really effective against the ball being trundled or skimmed along the ground. First-class cricket began, retrospectively, in 1772.A Game of Cricket at The Royal Academy Club in Marylebone Fields, now Regent's Park, depiction by unknown artist, c. 1790–1799

- **History of cricket (1772–1815) and History of English cricket (1816–1863)**

The game also underwent a fundamental change of organisation with the formation for the first time of county clubs. All the modern county clubs, starting with Sussex in 1839, were founded during the 19th century. No sooner had the first county clubs established themselves than they faced what amounted to "player action" as William Clarke created the travelling All-England Eleven in 1846. Though a commercial venture, this team did much to popularise the game in districts which had never previously been visited by high-class cricketers. Other similar teams were created and this vogue lasted for about thirty years. But the counties and MCC prevailed.

- **A cricket match at Darnall, Sheffield in the 1820s.**

The growth of cricket in the mid and late 19th century was assisted by the development of the railway network. For the first time, teams from a long distance apart could play one other without a prohibitively time-consuming journey. Spectators could travel longer distances to matches, increasing the size of crowds. Army units around the Empire had time on their hands, and encouraged the locals so they could have some entertaining competition. Most of the Empire embraced cricket, with the exception of Canada.

In 1864, another bowling revolution resulted in the legalisation of overarm and in the same year. W. G. Grace began his long and influential career at this time, his feats doing much to increase cricket's popularity. He introduced technical innovations which revolutionised the game, particularly in batting.

- **International cricket begins**

The first ever international cricket game was between the US and Canada in 1844. The match was played at the grounds of the St George's Cricket Club in New York.

- **The English team 1859 on their way to the US**

In 1859, a team of leading English professionals set off to North America on the first-ever overseas tour and, in 1862, the first English team toured Australia. Between May and October 1868, a team of Aboriginal Australians toured England in what was the first Australian cricket team to travel overseas.

- **The first Australian touring team (1878) pictured at Niagara Falls**

In 1877, an England touring team in Australia played two matches against full Australian XIs that are now regarded as the inaugural Test matches. The following year, the Australians toured England for the first time and the success of this tour ensured a popular demand for similar ventures in future. No Tests were played in 1878 but more soon followed and, at The Oval in 1882, the Australian victory in a tense finish gave rise to The Ashes.South Africa became the third Test nation in 1889.

- **National championships**

A significant development in domestic cricket occurred in 1890 when the official County Championship was constituted in England. Soon afterwards, in May 1894, the sport's first-class standard was officially defined. This organisational initiative has been repeated in other countries. Australia established the Sheffield Shield in 1892–93. Other national competitions to be established were the Currie Cup in South Africa, the Plunket Shield in New Zealand and the Ranji Trophy in India. The ICC re-defined first-class status in 1947 as a global concept.

The period from 1890 to the outbreak of the First World War has become one of nostalgia, ostensibly because the teams played cricket according to "the spirit of the game", but more realistically because it was a peacetime period that was shattered by the First World War. The era has been called The Golden Age of cricket and it featured numerous great names such as Grace, Wilfred Rhodes, C. B. Fry, Ranjitsinhji and Victor Trumper.

- **Balls per over**

During most of the 19th-century standard overs were made up of four deliveries. In 1889 five-ball overs were introduced in first-class cricket, with a move to generally use six-ball overs in 1900.

In the 20th-century, eight-ball overs were used at times in a number of countries, primarily Australia, where eight-balls were the standard over length between 1918/19 and 1978/79, South Africa and New Zealand. Since the 1979/80 Australian and New Zealand seasons, six balls per over have been used worldwide, and the most recent version of the Laws only permits six-ball overs.

- **Growth of international cricket**

Sid Barnes traps Lala Amarnath lbw in the first official Test between Australia and India at the MCG in 1948

The Imperial Cricket Conference was founded in 1909 with England, Australia and South Africa as the founder members. This aimed to regulate international cricket between the three sides, considered the only three of equal status at the time. West Indies were admitted as members in 1928, allowing them to play Test cricket against the other sides. New Zealand and India both became Test playing nations before World War II and Pakistan joined soon afterwards in 1952.

At the initial suggestion of Pakistan, the ICC was expanded to include non-Test playing countries from 1965, with Associate members being admitted. At the same time the organisation changed its name to the International Cricket Conference. The first limited-overs World Cups were played during the 1970s and Sri Lanka became the first

Associate member to be raised to Test playing status in 1982.

The international game continued to grow with the introduction of Affiliate Member status in 1984, a level of membership designed for sides with less history of playing cricket. In 1989 the ICC renamed itself the International Cricket Council. Zimbabwe became Full Members in 1992 and Bangladesh in 2000 before Afghanistan and Ireland were both admitted as Test sides in 2018, bringing the number of full members of the ICC to 12.

- **International cricket in South Africa from 1971 to 1981**

The greatest crisis to hit international cricket was brought about by apartheid, the South African policy of racial segregation. The situation began to crystallise after 1961 when South Africa left the Commonwealth of Nations and so, under the rules of the day, its cricket board had to leave the International Cricket Conference (ICC). Cricket's opposition to apartheid intensified in 1968 with the cancellation of England's tour to South Africa by the South African authorities, due to the inclusion in the England team of Basil D'Oliveira, a Cape Coloured player. In 1970, the ICC members voted to suspend South Africa indefinitely from international cricket competition.

Starved of top-level competition for its best players, the South African Cricket Board began funding so-called "rebel tours", offering large sums of money for international players to form teams and tour South Africa. The ICC's response was to blacklist any rebel players who agreed to tour South Africa, banning them from officially sanctioned international cricket. As players were poorly remunerated during the 1970s, several accepted the offer to tour South Africa, particularly players getting towards the end of their careers for which a blacklisting would have little effect.

The rebel tours continued into the 1980s but then progress was made in South African politics and it became clear that apartheid was ending. South Africa, now a "Rainbow Nation" under Nelson Mandela, was welcomed back into international sport in 1991.

- **World Series Cricket**

The money problems of top cricketers were also the root cause of another cricketing crisis that arose in 1977 when the Australian media magnate Kerry Packer fell out with the Australian Cricket Board over TV rights. Taking advantage of the low remuneration paid to players, Packer retaliated by signing several of the best players in the world to a privately run cricket league outside the structure of international cricket. World Series Cricket hired some of the banned South African players and allowed them to show off their skills in an international arena against other world-class players. The schism lasted only until 1979 and the "rebel" players were allowed back into established international cricket, though many found that their national teams had moved on without them. Long-term results of World Series Cricket have included the introduction of significantly higher player salaries and innovations such as coloured kit and night games.

- **Limited-overs cricket**

In the 1960s, English county teams began playing a version of cricket with games of only one innings each and a maximum number of overs per innings. Starting in 1963 as a knockout competition only, limited-overs cricket grew in popularity and, in 1969, a national league was created which consequently caused a reduction in the number of matches in the County Championship. The status of limited overs matches is governed by the official List A categorisation. Although many "traditional" cricket fans objected to the shorter form of the game, limited-overs cricket did have the advantage of delivering a result to spectators within a single day; it did improve cricket's appeal to younger or busier people; and it did prove commercially successful.

The first limited-overs international match took place at Melbourne Cricket Ground in 1971 as a time-filler after a Test match had been abandoned because of heavy rain on the opening days. It was tried simply as an experiment and to give the players some exercise, but turned out to be immensely popular. limited-overs internationals (LOIs or ODIs—one-day internationals) have since grown to become a massively popular form of the game, especially for busy people who want to be able to see a whole match. The International Cricket Council reacted to this development by organising the first Cricket World Cup in England in 1975, with all the Test-playing nations taking part.

- **Analytic and graphic technology**

Limited-overs cricket increased television ratings for cricket coverage. Innovative techniques introduced in coverage of limited-over matches were soon adopted for Test coverage. The innovations included presentation of in-depth statistics and graphical analysis, placing miniature cameras in the stumps, multiple usage of cameras to provide shots from several locations around the ground, high-speed photography and computer graphics technology enabling television viewers to study the course of a delivery and help them understand an umpire's decision.

In 1992, the use of a third umpire to adjudicate run-out appeals with television replays was introduced in the Test series between South Africa and India. The third umpire's duties have subsequently expanded to include decisions on other aspects of play such as stumpings, catches and boundaries. From 2011, the third umpire was being called upon to moderate review of umpires' decisions, including lbw, with the aid of virtual-reality tracking technologies (e.g., Hawk-Eye and Hot Spot), though such measures still could not free some disputed decisions from heated controversy.

- **21st-century cricket**

In June 2001, the ICC introduced a "Test Championship Table" and, in October 2002, a "One-day International Championship Table". As indicated by ICC rankings, the various cricket formats have continued to be a major competitive sport in most former British Empire countries, notably the Indian subcontinent, and new participants including the Netherlands. In 2017, the number of countries with full ICC membership was increased to twelve by the addition of Afghanistan and Ireland.

The ICC expanded its development programme, aiming to produce more national teams capable of competing at the various formats. Development efforts are focused on African and Asian nations, and on the United States. In 2004, the ICC Intercontinental Cup brought first-class cricket to 12 nations, mostly for the first time. Cricket's newest innovation is Twenty20, essentially an evening entertainment. It has so far enjoyed enormous popularity and has attracted large attendances at matches as well as good TV audience ratings. The inaugural ICC Twenty20 World Cup tournament was held in 2007. The formation of Twenty20 leagues in India – the unofficial Indian Cricket League, which started in 2007, and the official Indian Premier League, starting in 2008 – raised much speculation in the cricketing press about their effect on the future of cricket.

Printed by Libri Plureos GmbH in Hamburg, Germany